Love Letter
to Humanity

Love Letter to Humanity

You Are Love

Howard I. Westin

To order additional copies of this book, contact:
Xlibris Corporation
1-888-795-4274
www.Xlibris.com
Orders@Xlibris.com
18068

Contents

FOR ANNIE, MY WIFE, FRIEND, SOULMATE, &
COMPASSIONATE LOVER OF HUMANITY

ACKNOWLEDGEMENTS

SINCE SO MANY of you have been my teachers, it is impossible here to name all of you. For the immediate purposes of this letter, I am sure you will appreciate those whom I do acknowledge:

Thank you Sarah Miles, for introducing me to *A Course in Miracles* in 1986 while I was your pastor and you sensed my need for a deeper spiritual thrust.

Likewise Bishop Spong, for all your writings. It's been like returning to seminary and re-learning anew the Bible. Together with all the people of the Community Church of Lauderdale-By-The-Sea who allowed me the forum for preaching and teaching all of what you read in my *Love Letter to Humanity*.

To Patrisia for her painting, *The Light*, illustrative of my dream found on page 71. Jim Pollock's technical expertise and guidance assisted me to get my material camera ready for the publisher, Xlibris Corporation. John Dillard of Xlibris also greatly assisted in expediting my "Letter." Thank you, too, Michael Dropkin for your computer assistance.

Then all you perceptive reviewers whom I list alphabetically . . . the hours you invested in our friendship going over several drafts and offering me your wise suggestions, Wow! Thank you for all the energy and love you invested in editorializing.

TO: Dean Avary; David Avens; Alan Cohen; Sandra Cortez; W. Thomas Gossett, Jr.; Phil Hinton; Kirk Johnson; Don Martin; Harvey Martin (no relation); My esteemed mentor and colleague, the Rev. Jon Mundy; Barry Murphy; Chuck and Glenda Okerstrom; Robert Perry, the dean of all ACIM teachers; Ed Peterson; Jay Smith; John Soller, Sr.; Norm Wagy; and my sons, Mark, Tim, Rick and Bill.

And finally, Annie, for your partnership in this writing. All who know you realize you live what I write!

INTRODUCTION

IT'S THE SEASON of Christmas, 2002. Underneath and above and beyond, I hear the music and the words of *"Peace on Earth, Good Will among men,"* in spite of daily reminders of current and future wars.

For the past year, I have wanted to write. It's been a gradual thing; a gentle intuitive awareness that I must write. With retirement occurring June of 2002, the opportunity was ripe. Being an avid reader of almost every book available about the historical Jesus of Nazareth, and also a student of *A Course in Miracles*, I knew my subject would center on the teachings of each. What follows is a composite of my beliefs resulting from these resources.

Much of what I write here is autobiographical. It has been my privilege to wear a number of hats throughout my careers as lawyer, minister; also recreational violinist and golfer. You, as reader, will soon discover I bounce around somewhat. I write my *Love Letter to Humanity* to everyone and realize some might have trouble understanding portions of it. Stay with me please. I promise your patience will be rewarded! The message I wish to share? **Love Ultimately Is All There Is!** The emphasis of this letter is that we can't have "Peace on Earth and good will among men," **unless Love Itself is recognized, taught, and practiced as the only Reality.**

Some senior citizens may not agree with my views because all they have experienced, for most of their lives, is war and the threat of war. World peace is considered to be an unattainable dream since "evil nations" exist. That implies that some nations are "not evil" giving rise to prideful statements such as "My country right or wrong." And then, there are many religious leaders who make pronouncements about "just wars," as though a Creator favors some nations, peoples, races, and sexes over others. God takes sides?

It has never been easy to alter significantly a belief system that defines one's life. "Why change now?" my generation asks. "We have done our best!" And, indeed, most of us have. We have reason to celebrate raising decent families and providing many significant contributions to society and that includes unselfish Love.

The younger generations, predominantly, are among those questioning some of these world-views. I will try to answer their many concerns by relating the events of our lives from within those inexpressible **experiences of Love** common to all of us.

As one recognizing a universal (catholic) church only as that conforms to this very essence of **Love**, I constantly refer to history's **most unique teacher of Love,** Jesus of Nazareth, a Galilean peasant of the Middle East. His teachings of **Love** are reflected both in the picturesque language of Aramaic and the Greek translations of the New Testament. More has been written and proclaimed about him than any other man.

I also believe we live simultaneously in two qualitatively opposite worlds. Jesus of Nazareth described this as *being **in** the world, yet not **of** it.* The physical world is where we seem to live 99.99% of the time; but then, there exists .01% of 'timelessness' in which we experience everything as indescribably beautiful, peaceful, and joyous! (Heaven on Earth?)

Marcus Borg, Professor of Religion and Culture at Oregon State University, refers to this state of timelessness as a *mystical* understanding of God. He writes,

"Central to such . . . are three features. 1) God, or the "sacred," is ineffable, beyond all words and concepts. 2) God is not "a being," but a nonmaterial layer or level or dimension of reality that both permeates everything and at the same time is more than everything. 3) God can be experienced. *The sacred is not primarily an article of belief, but an element of experience"* (Italics mine.)

Should my letter continue to hold your interest, you may recognize a circularity to its construction and content. By this, I don't mean to be leading you around in a circle, but rather in a spiral. Perhaps you will experience a cumulative progression of thought. This letter is an appeal to every one of Earth's citizens to rediscover the ways of Peace taught by all the Masters including Jesus. It is not meant to be sectarian but I do write primarily from within my experiences of Christianity, whose student I have been all my life.

Bishop John Shelby Spong, in a recent essay, concluded it with these prophetic words: "A free nation, no matter how powerful, cannot finally defend itself against those who are willing to die in order to inflict pain on the ones they think of as their enemies. We may well conquer the world with our power only to discover that we have become vulnerable to decades of terrorists acts which will suck the very life out of the freedom that made America possible. If we do not find some unity in our humanity, then the tribal claims of competing nations will finally destroy civilization itself." (From a column published by Agora Media.com. entitled *"The War with Iraq: Can We Find Unity in Our Humanity."*)

Many of us cry out in unison with you, Bishop Spong, in order that we truly have "Peace on Earth and Good Will among Men."

CHAPTER ONE

YOU ARE LOVE

I WRITE THIS letter to you whomever and wherever you are. It's personal but obviously, not private. What others think of you, by name, sex, race, ethnicity, or age matters not. I wish to communicate with you that **we together can share Our Love and bring Peace to each other within this world.**

Why not? Is not Love what each one seeks? Not a love with conditions attached, but a Love that transcends distinctions, extending without limitation along, through, and within our Selves! And so I ask, "Why is it then that, since we seek Love, we seldom experience it? Could it be we've been too restrictive in our search?" Well, here's some terrific news you and I should consider: **Love *Is* our very Selves,** surrounding us anywhere and everywhere we are.

Yet, if we can sing "Love Makes The World Go Round;" and "All You Need Is Love;" then why should we have to experience fear so much of the time? A recent documentary film by Michael Moore based on the tragic classroom shootings in Littleton, Colorado, shows how **fear dominates the minds of Americans.** In his film, *"Bowling for Columbine,"* Moore indicates that the media and many political leaders fan the fires of fear among us.

Our most unforgettable teachers remind us, though, that we **can** learn to counteract these fears and practice living more frequently in a *present* moment of our choice. We **can connect** with Love by rediscovering **within ourselves** *stillness* beyond words, thoughts, and external distractions. Like stumbling upon a diamond ring while walking along the beach (our minds being totally blank) and then . . . something beautifully strange happens! We call it the **'aha' experience.** Admittedly, such is rarely experienced in today's world.

In this letter, I'd like to remind you of how your own unique experiences of those wonderful present moments materialize. Is it not like being on a "journey without distance;" of time itself seemingly standing still? I want to convince you of what you already know but have forgotten. I want you to recall and experience daily **Who You Are: Your actual and virtual Existence or Beingness As Love. Awesome! Both the fact of and the experience of You *As* Love!**

Every time I enter an elevator, for example, and see another person and then say, "Hello, how are you?" I purposely observe what happens. Either the other person will smile or answer with something nice, or he/she will appear shut-off from communications. I'll honor whatever state of mind is reflected, and respond accordingly. Where there is the slightest opening of a smile or a word, I will recognize that moment with gratitude **and** *feel* what is taking place. I have learned not to dismiss that exchange too quickly because we have actually shared **Love Itself**. We are mirroring *Who We both Are* . . . **The Beingness of Love**. Each of us **is** partaking in the Oneness of Love. Although this may be experienced for only a second, it is enough to register.

A jogger approaches, intent on saving his breath, and actually nods his head and smiles, despite the challenge of physical exertion. It may be he is in the "zone" and so much inside an "inner realm" that only a smile could possibly come my way. This I receive as a gift of Love. There is plenty more of this coming all day long if I'm alert and receptive. You also can become the beneficiary and giver of this, Love's tender and soft warmth, as you cultivate a discipline and a willingness to manifest **It!** It is how we begin to realize time as standing still. We recognize how **giving and receiving are identical within this zone of Beingness.** We are aware of something beautiful taking place in a present moment. **What a Present!** And it's as free as the air we breathe: **"Love is in the Air."**

When I said, "giving and receiving are the same," here's what I meant. As we give to others, we receive more than their gratitude, because, deep in our hearts, the act of giving acknowledges a *feeling* we share forever; there is gain and never loss. Love is a permanent possession. **You are Love and that You are forever!**

It cannot be said often enough that you and I have the best of Teachers within us. Yet we have not been meaningfully introduced to **this Mentor** for any sustained period of seconds, let alone minutes. To maintain a connection with my inner Truth, my Mentor, I often repeat a helpful mantra several times a day: *"This Holy Instant I give to You. Be You in charge; for I would follow Your direction which gives me Peace!" (From A Course* in *Miracles).* Please note that, although we constantly receive instruction from external resources, that mode of 'learning' is not necessarily **Knowledge.**

Knowledge is an inner awareness. Knowledge, Power, and Presence; each are aspects of our virtual Identity. We do not acquire these Traits in the conventional manner of learning. We were born into this world *already* possessing Knowledge, (Omniscience); Power, (Omnipotence); and, Presence, (Omnipresence). That is referred to in the Bible as being *"Created in the Image of God".* This is recognized with *feelings* of awe. It is Knowledge beyond words. It is descriptive of our Real Selves as God's Creation! You **are** Knowledge, Power, and Presence. **God is Love, and so are You.**

Obviously, I interpret the Bible a bit differently than some. For instance, in the stories about Isaac's sons we, like Jacob's older brother Esau, carelessly and thoughtlessly trade off the above "Traits or

Inheritances" for material things. (Esau was entitled to his father's entire estate under the law yet, famished with hunger, he gave up his preferred right of inheritance to younger brother Jacob simply for some stew.) Is that not as ridiculous as a very young child trading a new bicycle for an ice cream cone? But who would expect a child of three to have any idea of the vastly greater value of the bike? "Instant gratification," unfortunately, typifies what many foolishly seek today. This is descriptive of the "Me Generation." However, why should we be thinking "me, me." We own **IT all, right now**! Love doesn't lack a thing. Question is, do we really understand this?

Jesus of Nazareth challenged his listeners to be consciously aware of Who they Really *are* within the Universe. He taught them to *Be* who they were created to *Be*. He said, *"**Be** as perfect as your Creator/ Mother/Father!"* We know and understand Who we truly are whenever and as often as we continually cultivate an inner awareness of our original Presence, Power, and Knowledge. **This is Knowledge beyond thinking**. Your repeated reentry into the Realm of Love happens as often as you choose and, usually, to your pleasant surprise, at times you least expect. The **Realm of Love Is Beingness with Your "Heavenly" Father. What's His is Yours**!

Each one of you is my Teacher. You have enabled me to become a violinist, lawyer, and minister. Some of you have taught me to play golf, which I compare with Life. Have you played this game? Anyone playing soon recognizes "**who**" or "**W**ho" she is the very moment a shot is made or missed! Unlike most sports there is no way a golfer should blame or credit someone else for the result of a shot. This does account for some very strange behavior of tossed clubs and weird body language! So what? Well, playing golf is like living your life. The way you handle a tough golf shot parallels how you respond to adversity. Your ability to respond from within your awareness of Love extends to other players. They are grateful to you for the gift of your gentle patience.

Top players have psychologists for coaches because they know that their performance is dependent upon the peace existing within an inner state of mind. Why not make it our momentary decision to Live Life as it is intended for ones so talented? Two of the world's best golfers, Tiger Woods and Annika Sorenstam, certainly must attribute their success to the disciplines of Beingness: (The focus of Mind, Body, Strength, and Soul equally contributing to who they are.) I am positive they readily acknowledge their Coach as being within them! It's very obvious they love Life and Golf.

When we made our grand entry into this beautiful world, our teachers were waiting for us. Parents and relatives and caretakers had their own ideas as to who we should be. It is in such manner, therefore, that I define our egos: **a bundle of beliefs, we perceive as our identity**.

"You are beautiful and handsome" or, "an ugly duckling." "You keep getting in the way and are a bother." "You talk too much!" or "Don't speak unless spoken to!" "Why can't you get the same high grades as your sister?" "Wish you were never born!" We get the picture. It doesn't take long before we accept those perceptions as identities of who we are. By the time we are teenagers, we actually flee one set of "image makers" and seek approval from other enhancers of ego: our peers. They're attracted to us for the same reason. "Misery loves company."

Some of us are more fortunate. Most parent-teachers tried to nourish us to respect ourselves. They corrected us in meaningful terms most times we strayed. They loved enough to introduce us to certain avenues allowing for our own unique experience of **Love Itself.** I'll try to illustrate this in my own early experience of life.

Although reared in a strict home, I eventually understood how much pain and sacrifice my parents endured in order to encourage me in acquiring a healthier self-image. Eric and Freda Westin emigrated from Sweden in the early 1920's. America, our great land of opportunity, enabled them to build a home and have a family. Then came the depression of the 30's. Instead of standing in bread lines, they scrubbed floors in the Stambaugh Building in downtown Youngstown, Ohio, following Sunday morning church services. The few extra dollars they had to spend beyond food, clothing and shelter went towards private violin lessons for brother George and me. Doesn't that indicate selfless Love?

Think of it. Today, I can pick up a violin any place and create music to my heart's content. Because of

Dad and Mom's extended Love, I can experience my Self as a violinist. That, in addition to those other talents you, my Teachers, have elicited from me **contributing to the realization that I am not, ultimately, just an "ego."**

It requires persistence to re-discover that healthiest of Self Images Jesus of Nazareth viewed in us. We are literally "disciples" of those teachers we admire the most, whether they are parents, coaches or philosophers. As disciples or followers of Jesus' teachings, we were called, *"Children of God" and "Light Of The World"* no matter whom we are. (Incidentally, "discipleship" is the acceptance of the same discipline or teaching as that of a Master Teacher.) And so Jesus, in teaching us to be "Light," was reminding us about our essential Oneness with one another, with him, and also with the Creator. For the many accepting this higher esteem for themselves and others, this world reappears wonderfully different . . . different enough to **Love and enjoy** immensely.

Many years pass before most of us comprehend our more challenging problems. Counselors are of some help. Most of them take us on trips into the past so we might discover the causes of our behavior. There are seekers, though, who take a more adventurous route and re-enter many times daily that Realm where the Answer for all problems is given. This Answer amplifies an awesome awareness of **Who We Are as Love;** and then, we recognize we have no problems. **Thinking we are separate from God, our Source, is our only problem; while the**

experience of Oneness within this Universe and with our Creator is the Answer!

The Realm of Love has several names. All the great Teachers agree that Love is experienced as a timeless existence of the Now or the Precious Present. Does this sound unworldly? Well, in a certain sense, it is! Jesus told many stories about a Realm, or Empire, he called the Kingdom of God. He painted vividly alive pictures about living on our beautiful planet Earth, and yet simultaneously, not being of it. As this letter unfolds, I continually allude to this.

Regrettably, Jesus' teachings became so distorted that the religion purportedly organized in his name hardly looks like the "Christianity" he taught. There are those who proclaim a message of fear and hatred as though this originated from Jesus, who himself was truly a compassionate Jewish peasant. Any un-churched person who views Christian TV or listens to bombastic radio warnings of hell and damnation misses Jesus' message: *"You are Loved, and in You God is well pleased."* Since my background is that of the church, readers of other traditions will appreciate my bias. However, this letter is intended for all peoples. You, whoever you are, can recognize this from within the teachings of your own unique Masters. **They too accept the Oneness of Creation!** Humanity has a common history.

God has neither gender nor a split personality! **The Author of Creation is the Beingness of Love. You are Love.** That is the good news all religions teach, once they get beyond those false interpretations men and women make of "gods" from out of their own imaginings. It is within this context that I understand the commandment, *"Thou shalt have no other gods before me;"* **no idols beyond the experience of Love/God.**

CHAPTER TWO

LOVE HAS *NO* OPPOSITE

Y OU MAY BE reading something different here about Love. Love *is* experienced during and after suffering physical and emotional pain is it not? Although in this world, **Love appears to be the opposite of fear,** how is it that some of us have no fear of suffering and death? The fact is that deep within us there can be strong resistance to Love. Have you wondered why this is so? The answer is simple. Most of our lives we have been taught "success" belongs to those possessing the most things. Real estate is real, and when you're dead you're dead! Jesus taught the opposite. Since you already own everything, why struggle to acquire what you already possess? **You don't lack a thing.** As for death, there is no death, only Life after life. That teaching is resisted because we have not been taught to understand otherwise. The attraction to 'things' we have made **is** almost irresistible!

We haven't been taught that our struggles for position and power are needless. This is too good to be true. We live our lives doubting this and other related truths taught by Jesus and other master teachers. There is embedded deeply within our beings a competitive and unconscious drive to "succeed." **Succeed in what?** Alas, our energies are being devoted mostly to what ultimately is *no-thing!* We are envious of the rewards acquired by strong-willed, powerful, possessors of real estate and things. **Small wonder fear arises within us whenever loss of such 'valued' things is threatened.** This poses the question, "What do I really value?" So why not pause a moment and think, "What *do* I value?" If "Love is all there is," what else could really be of value?

Love is always there, gently suggesting we are on the wrong track most of the time. "But that is insane!" we cry. Our entire conduct of life has been otherwise. To be told that we should change over to an entirely opposite lifestyle is somewhat "fearful." Gently, persistently, Love whispers, *"Fear not, I have overcome this world (of fear) for you"* and, "You *teach only Love for that **is** What You Are!"* (*From A Course In Miracles*) and then, it may occur to us . . . sometime . . . that Love does encompass all that *is* Real; there is **no fear that we need fear!** Fear, in the ultimate sense, does not exist. We may still cry out, "You've got to be kidding!" Love answers again, reassuring us there is *no*-thing for us to fear! Things come and go. They are made by man and have no permanency. "Here today and gone tomorrow."

A Course in Miracles states: **"Nothing real can**

**be threatened. Nothing unreal exists. Herein lies
the peace of God**." (ACIM, 2nd Ed., Introduction.)
Think about that would you please? Pause a moment
and reflect on what that is saying. Then say to
yourself, "Fear need not paralyze me; it, being
unreal, does not ultimately exist!" God is Love, and
within that Love, all that is Real Exists. What God
Creates is endless; It is forever, eternal. Furthermore,
what man Co-creates together with God are
Extensions of Love. Some people compose Music or
create Art, which, some of it, are also Extensions of
Universal and Timeless Love! Such are not "things"
for they Re-Present Creation Itself. We either co-
Create what is Eternal or make things of limited
duration.

Granted, it is not easy to accept Love's invitation
and live Life according to **Its** directions. It is not easy
to persistently and consciously live in Love. Doing so
requires the discipline and repetitive practice that an
athlete in training must exert. That's a lot of work!
"Right, Annika and Tiger?" Theologians use the term
"cheap Grace" for those who take for granted their
status of Oneness with God. In Truth, Grace or Love **is
freely granted to the entirety of Creation.**

This is good news and **Its** conscious realization
by us, **Its** acknowledgement, comes about every
moment we choose to **experience It.** That's the
discipline we need practice. The only "cost" to us is
our willingness to accept God's Acceptance of us just
as we are. What **is** amazing, we need do nothing if we
so choose, **since sooner or "later" we will 'wake up'.**
What's left for us to fear?

We **can** cultivate this discipline anytime we **will to Be**. Why not now? I admittedly am an impatient person. I am a rabid sports fan. Regretfully, I confess that when driving in traffic, I have manifested a certain form of road rage. As a die-hard sports fan, I have become a candidate for a lynch mob and the other team has, in my wrongful state of mind, become the enemy; my mortal foe: "Hit 'em again! Hit 'em again harder!" With what consistency do I teach about Love-Beingness? Where is *my* discipline of Love to counteract that fear, anger, rage, and insanity? Where's my patience? These certainly are relevant and pertinent questions.

There is a way through it all if we are game. What I do when my stomach feels 'tied up' with lead weights and my nerves feel frazzled, I . . . stop, look, and listen, and pay attention to what is going on within my body. I actually see the knots and quivering nerve fibers in my inner body. Then, I listen to my Teacher tell me "Well done, Howie," and actually experience a release of those negative feelings. This is healing. This is Grace!

Nor does this require external help. It's entirely an inside job. With gratitude, I accept the Peace which envelops me and strips away another layer of misguided thinking. People who have known me for several years tell me that I'm nicer to be around, and I agree. Their comments encourage me to travel a more exciting road from the dead end streets of past patterns. I feel a sense of Real accomplishment; I'm learning to live peacefully. **I am also learning to live fearlessly and confident as to my purpose in**

**living life. I am learning that Love, indeed, has no
Real opposition.**

So can you, once you get in touch with your inner
Guide. Accept the power of living Now. Don't wait
for something outside of you to come to your rescue.
You could wait beyond any conscious desire to
change for the better. (Rest homes are filled with
people who no longer care to live.)

What I am writing is contrary to what many teach.
The "something outside of you" can be any organized
tribunal claiming exclusive authority over what you
must think and believe in order to be "saved";
otherwise you are ' damned', exiled, or at best-
shunned. It is one of my primary intentions in writing
this letter, to refute the general impression that
certain churches are exclusively entitled to the
identity-name of "Christian."

**There do exist, thankfully, many Churches
experiencing everyone within and without as a
Family of Families living Life together in a
Communion of Love.** That, in my opinion, is the
Church which reflects the actual Teachings of Jesus
of Nazareth; whether or not it is called "Christian."
The fact is that the earliest disciples of Jesus were
called, **"Followers of the Way."** And, get this . . . they
were peacefully, and joyfully fearless. They saw the
world through different eyes.

**Not all of us who follow Jesus, the Galilean
Teacher, accept as definitive,** the statement: *"Believe
in God's only Son Jesus as the sacrificial lamb who*

offers His Divine Life in payment for your sins and therefore you are assured of going to heaven." (More on this in Chapters Eight and Nine)

If the above sentence reflects your belief so be it. My purpose is not to change your beliefs as only you can decide this. I merely advise there **is** a different way of viewing this. There is a Way of Peace and "no fear." The Jesus I recognize as my Friend and Teacher, Jesus, the Galilean peasant, who dared to live fully a Life of Love, taught that Heaven and the Reign of God are the same as the **present experience of God in us. God is in us and we are in God.** What else is there in the Universe?

"Heaven" is not a "future" land where St. Peter opens or shuts the gate of entry. It is the turf we are standing on this very moment. Wherever and whenever one joins together with another in the name of Love, that event is **"*Christian.*"** The *Church I* write about is not an exclusive organization. It includes every seeker and doer of Love! Incidentally, the literal meaning of the word 'catholic' is universal or all-inclusiveness. Catholic includes all of Creation. (And, by the way, there is no "hell," either.)

Your choice of heaven or hell is a present moment choice. So powerful are your mind and will. Maybe you might think of it this way. We, at any moment, can be of a wrong frame of mind or, of One Mind with the Creator. Because Love, ultimately, has no opposite, I encourage you to ask your inner Guide to **Re-Mind You of Who You Are as a Son/Daughter of God.** This process of Re-Minding is also known as the correction of one's thinking; atonement or **"At-One-ment!"**

It has been my privilege over the years, to study what many past or current scholars of science and religion write concerning self-improvement. You may have come to similar conclusions based upon reading a lot of "self-help" books. I do recognize, however, that reading and doing are not always consistent. It makes sense that if our unconscious habits of behavior have been etched into the fiber of our self-identities (egos) over all the previous years, it is bound to require persistent and deliberate effort to change these established ways of thinking and doing.

We are afraid to change when that appears "inconvenient" or because we don't have the time. Why? Since it may take a long time to correct behavior and ingrained habits, we **doubt ourselves**, questioning our ability to change. Are we that lazy? Or has someone or some "thing" convinced us we are incapable of change, causing us to doubt or fear our own innate Power of Love. Listen carefully. Love, when invited by us, erases all fear and doubt.

Anyone who wants to lose weight or quit smoking knows what the odds are in doing a 180 degree shift of one's lifestyle. What is required is desire and willingness. That's the rub. We doubt ourselves. We doubt and even resist Love's Power within us. Like those who live in a dream, we wait for our personal genie to do it for us. What's the difference between that and expecting the organizational church or some magical marvel drug to be the guarantor of our "salvation?"

Only We can do it. There are no magic wands or fairy godmothers. The good news is there is no "thing" to fear or doubt. Our healing is already an accomplished fact. It's a "done deal"! I suggest this prayer: **Thank You, Holy Spirit** (*our inner Teacher*), **for teaching We are, each one of us, One within Oneness.**

One of my favorite Teachers, Jon Mundy, author, lecturer, and publisher, expresses it beautifully, "Each one can tune into either one of two radio stations *WGOD* or *WEGO* (edge God out.) These two voices constantly vie for attention. How do we tell the difference? The first voice to speak usually is the loudest and noisiest. We can be sure that one is our ego. Our Real Teacher (Guide, God, Holy Spirit, Allah, Jesus, Buddha, or Higher Self, etc.) is peaceful and soothing. Getting past the noise in our cluttered minds, into the stillness of Beingness (our True Self), we can hear a calm inner Voice gently correcting our misperceptions. With It also comes Will, Grace and Wisdom, enabling us to Be and Do." **Did not Jesus teach that all we need do is ask, and we would receive an answer?**

The entity called ego is fictitious. It, nevertheless, seems to "manufacture" doubt and fear within us and can be considered "vicious" at times. St. Paul describes this condition vividly in his letter to the Roman church back in the first century A.D. (I've taken the liberty to interpret.)

"So I find this law at work: When I want to do good, evil is right there with me. For in my inner being I delight in God's law; but I see another law at work (ego?) in the members of my body, waging war against the law of my mind and making me a prisoner of the law of sin (ego?) at work within my members. What a wretched man I am!

Who will rescue me from this body (ego?) of death? Thanks be to God-through Jesus (, the) Christ our Lord!" (parentheses mine) Rom. 7:21ff)

In reality, we are doing this to ourselves. Like any imaginary fairy or demon that we conjure up, so is the ego with which we identify 99.99% of the time. Try a little experiment. Quiet your mind for a few seconds. Visualize a river. You are sitting on its bank and several boats are passing gently downstream. Think of these boats as floating thoughts. Just watch them. Watch whatever thought predominates and occupies your thinking. Like a scientist looking through a microscope, **you are an observer.** Just think. You, the observer, can visualize yourself thinking thoughts! You are observing your thinking self. **You** realize that you are so much more than a physical and sensual self. **You are Beingness Itself! You are Love! You are Knowledge, Power, and Presence. Awesome!**

Station **WGOD.** Re-Minds you that **You as You have been Created, are Love Itself.** Words cannot convey **Love as It Is;** *words are but symbols of symbols of Reality.* Put it this way: Music and Poetry, and some Holy Scriptures, are but one symbol away from Reality. In a certain sense, Silence and Reality are the same. But most of our conversations reflect only the repeated thoughts of others. Such words rarely emerge consciously from one's creative Self. They are mundane, second-handed, unconscious, mechanical communications. (At that, quite a bit boring.)

Let's illustrate. When I play the violin, I may read and play notes written by the composer, or play "by heart" and allow the music to flow. The phenomenon called jazz is playing from the soul together with like-Minded musicians. It is possible, with the written notes being played, for an 80-piece symphony orchestra to **Be** under the spell of both composer and conductor. Each musician is simultaneously Being in the Now! Such has been my experience while playing in symphony orchestras. **It can Be** the Oneness of a Chorale group or congregation in union with *Spirit* singing and extending Love's Presence among, within, and throughout each and all of us within a timeless and present Now!

As a speaker, orator, preacher, professor, musician, or newscaster shares an insight of the heart, and transcends the written script, we may experience him or her as Being in the Now. When we are listening simultaneously to the same Teacher, *societal changes are possible.* We describe certain fearless people as prophets, seers, or inspired leaders when they express this Charisma of Being. Within us lay the same greatness. Within the **Oneness of Love** we are empowered to celebrate and extend a **Realm of Peace having no opposition**. "Know Thyself," so say the sages. I would paraphrase this and say **Know Thyself as Love! There can be no fear when you are living as, from, and within Love Itself.** What else in Creation is there?

CHAPTER THREE

JESUS AND HIS
FATHER/ABBA

S INCE YOU HAVE read this far, I congratulate
you! It has taken me seventy-four years to
begin to understand what you just read! It appears
you also want to become more of **Love** and expand
and express **It**. The Universe patiently 'awaits' our
responsible participation in perpetuating and
extending **Love** on planet Earth.

In this letter, I seek to write about a *human Jesus
of Nazareth*, a Jewish Galilean peasant, addressing
society from the perspective of Spirit; not organized
religion. His teachings declared that God, whom he
called Abba (Daddy, literally), is totally present
within Creation, and that includes every one of us.
God is within us! (Emanuel) That is Jesus' message
pure and simple. Mostly all else which has been
handed down to us since Jesus' day are the

interpretations of men; some of them true, much of it distorted or mistranslated.

Not everything we read in the recognized Gospels of the New Testament are Jesus' actual thoughts and words. Jesus of Nazareth may have spoken Greek but his primary language was Aramaic. This **presents imagery** unfamiliar to the Western mind but natural to the mind of the Easterner. Much of Aramaic is impossible to express adequately in English!

From the Yonan Codex Foundation writings (*Enlightenment From The Aramaic*) we read that, "Aramaic was the language of the Persian Empire, which stretched from the Mediterranean to the Great Wall of China for more than a thousand years before and after Jesus' birth. Its phonics is the language of Mohammed and the Koran. Its symbols appear upon the bricks lying in the plain near Babylon (modern Iraq,) and it is the language of the Dead Sea Scrolls."

Neil Douglas-Klotz, Ph.D., writes in his insightful book *The Hidden Gospel*, that

> "Scholars have also acknowledged in recent years that early Christian roots, not only reach back to Jewish spirituality, but also extend forward in time into Islam. According to Catholic scholar, Hans Kung, and others, some of the earliest views of Jesus (for instance, Jesus as the adopted, rather than the exclusive "Son of God") were preserved in early Islam. In this sense,

Kung has written that Islam poses a challenge for Christians as "A reminder of their own past."

"These perspectives allow us, perhaps for the first time in Western history, to begin to see Jesus as neither an orthodox Christian nor a Jew, but as a teacher influenced by the spirituality of the Middle East in general — as what I call a "native Middle Eastern" person . . . . For this reason, **looking at Jesus' words in Aramaic reveals the** Spirituality of his teachings in light of the Middle Eastern tradition **as a whole.** Jesus may indeed have been influenced by the Hellenistic (Greek) culture present in certain areas of Palestine, but the overwhelming numbers of people in his audience were not Greek speakers. In addition, people 'heard' the words of Jesus, rather than read them. In the oral tradition that followed him, people repeated and meditated upon his sayings and stories in a circular, spiritual way; not a linear, theological, or Western historical one." (Darkening mine.)

The Gospel of Mark, according to most scholars, was written about forty years after Jesus' death. It provides a partial foundational resource for the Gospels of Matthew and Luke written about a decade later. These writers wrote and thought from within a Greek, or Western world-view. If you think about it, it's not easy to accurately translate from one language to another. How much more difficult, then, to retain the sense of the original when a third, fourth or even fifth language is involved.

What we read in many renditions of the Bible is possibly five steps removed from what Jesus might have said if we include a progression of Aramaic, Greek, Latin, German, and English. Jesus, purportedly, did not write down anything of what he taught. There are no such writings existing. His Aramaic sayings, aphorisms and parables were repeated by word of mouth for several decades and, years later, recorded by scribes. The original Aramaic transcriptions are not available.

The oldest existing copies of the Greek translations are, at best, 3rd and 4th Century documents. Significantly, the oldest existing copies of Aramaic are dated 160 A.D. What the church teaches in and through its doctrines and creeds **are** the later interpretations of men.

Some poets, musicians, artists or writers transpose and compose Truth from within Beingness. Are not you and I able to interpret directly from **WGOD** and transform Truth from within Beingness Itself.? Why not? **We are Love. We are Spirit!** Although we are choosing to have a physical experience on planet Earth we remain what we are: **Spirit!** Like "Popeye, the Sailor Man," "I yam what I yam 'cause I yam what I yam."

Some of us have pursued concurrently the practices of Law and Ordained Ministry. It was a shock to family, colleagues, and friends when I took leave of the legal scene and entered seminary to become a Lutheran pastor. While being interviewed by the seminary president as to why I so drastically desired to change my life-style, disrupting my family etc., he chided me and said, "Howard, you really don't know very much theology."

In retrospect, he was right. Before the four-year intensive studies were completed I realized that when I entered the seminary, my understanding of the Bible (how and when it was written and to whom, etc.) was decidedly limited. At best, it was that of a 12-year old confirmation student and equivalent to that of most church members today. That changed considerably over the next four years and continues to evolve.

We dutifully try to understand what our ministers want us to believe. Clearly, for most of us, ours is *a faith in the faith of the church*: its doctrines, creeds, and biblical interpretations. We don't think it necessary to question anything. Our trust is in these, our learned teachers, to share what they understand the Bible to say about Jesus and that is that. No more questions please.

It is noticeably strange, is it not, that the Doctrine of the Trinity, as interpreted by many theologians receives so very little emphasis **as to the role of Spirit**. **Theology**, the study of God—yes; . . . **Christology**, the study of God's Son, the Christ—yes; . . . . but what of *Spiritology* and Its study? I have often questioned why it doesn't get "equal billing". Jesus' teachings centered on **Spirit** equally as much as **Father and Son.** (The Eastern Churches have recognized this historically.)

Nevertheless, the experience of laymen as they relate to clergy is not much different than what occurs in their visits to physicians or lawyers. We ask all of them to tell us what to do. Most of the words they use we fail to grasp. We trust they know what they are saying and advising until an adverse result causes us to doubt their credibility. Many current messengers of the church are increasingly losing their credibility. Some misrepresent Jesus, the Teacher, **as a sort of "third" being irrelevantly remote from who he truly is.** Honestly, how do you relate to a "God-man" unless you also Are One?

Nowhere in this letter will you find references to Jesus, the Christ, unless a comma is inserted between Jesus, and Christ. That is a tremendously important distinction. **The title Christ is synonymous with Holy Spirit; Presence of God; or the Annointed One.** I do not worship the *human being* known historically as Jesus of Nazareth. But I do worship, in awe, the ***Beingness of the Christ within Jesus,*** just as I hold in awe the Christ I see and meet in you daily. It is ***Jesus, the Christ.*** Think about this next very carefully: *Paul, the Christ?* Why not? Did not Paul say, *"I can do all things in Christ who strengthens me?"*

And did not Jesus teach that his mother and brothers and sisters are you and I, as we do the will of **our** Father? Can we not take him at his word? After all, **Jesus' Father is also "Our Father!"** Jesus is content to be our elder brother and certainly not some distant deity sitting on a throne on cloud nine somewhere up there. He specifically told his followers not to call him "Lord" since "Only our Father in heaven is Lord." Matthew records Jesus as saying, *"Do not call anyone on earth 'father' for you have one Father, and He is in Heaven. Nor are you to be called 'teacher,' for you have one Teacher, the Christ."* (*Matt. 23:9,10*)

I don't believe Jesus thought himself to be different from other human beings. He understood himself and each one of us to be God's children. Not one of us is special in God's eyes unless we are all of us equally so. When Jesus taught that we should Love one another he included our enemies. His were not just words about Love. He valued every person he met and that included some people we would avoid like the plague.

His concept of forgiveness is also beyond the practice of most. In effect, forgiveness, as we usually think of it, means that someone has harmed us and therefore we have been victimized. We will not forget what happened. ("I can forgive but not forget!") Since we are such "good" people, we will release them. "But, you better not do this again!" Jesus' views are radically different. If you don't **believe** you have been victimized, then there is nothing to forgive.

You **are** strong and there is no need for defense. What he meant about turning the other cheek or going an extra mile is that we **are** invulnerable to attack. "Hey, this is crazy. Put that man away!" That is exactly what happened. Such talk gets one into trouble. Jesus taught **defensiveness** to be **weakness** and **defenselessness strength**. "Picking up one's cross and following him" meant living from the same center of Love as did he. Clearly, his teachings are opposite from the thinking of today's world and community leaders. Refreshing to our Spirit, though, can be those we remember **living the Way of Jesus, the Christ, a Way of Love and Peace**! Gandhi and Martin Luther King Jr. come readily to mind.

"Gandhi, you say?" Gandhi, a Hindu, had memorized the entire New Testament! How many "Christians" can say that? When E. Stanley Jones, the noted Methodist missionary to India, asked him to proclaim publicly he was a Christian, Gandhi replied, "Give us your Christ; keep your Christianity!" Millions have followed Love's non-violent ways as taught by Jesus. Read Gandhi's autobiography. Defensive weapons? India won its Independence from Great Britain without resorting to violence. Who needs weaponry in the defense of Truth? Truth stands its own ground well enough, thank you. Truth and Love can withstand each and every instance of fear and attack. Practice this and you will understand who the historical Jesus of Nazareth was and what he taught and lived. I listen from within my being to Jesus' voice saying,

" . . . *Think of it this way: I am here only to be truly helpful.*

I am here to represent Him Who sent me. I do not have to worry about what to say or what to do, because He Who sent me will direct me. I am content to be wherever He wishes, knowing He goes there with me. I will be healed as I let Him teach me to heal."

(A Course in Miracles, 2ndEd. T 2. V.1)

CHAPTER FOUR

LET'S GET REAL ABOUT AND WITH JESUS!

JESUS OF NAZARETH was a radical and practical Teacher of Love. Small wonder his message was watered down. Nevertheless, the core of his teachings has changed the thinking of many, many contemporaries and countless thousands since. What he teaches is not impossible for us to implement, as some theologians have suggested. It **can** and **will** eventually be adopted by millions of us with an increasing desire to challenge the thinking of the rest of us. My purpose in this chapter is for us to reconsider who the "real historical Jesus" was. At the very least, *let's get real* about what we can learn about him and what he was actually teaching.

"Impossible possibility" or "Dream The Impossible Dream" — "Come on Westin, get real!" To which I strongly urge — **"Yes**, let's get **Real!"** By now, you are either irritated with my capitalizing some words, or you appreciate that Real and real, as I am using them, partake of two complementary dimensions. **To paraphrase Jesus, we are in the world of 'realness' and of the Realm of Realness simultaneously.** There is so much more to see and hear than what we are accustomed to experience.

Jesus lived in an Aramaic world where "heaven and earth" were, **in a Real sense, Oneness.** Again, I refer to the insightful writings of Neil Douglas-Klotz from *The Hidden Gospel:*

> "Our usual Western concepts of God and the sacred are only a partial view of Sacred Unity in the Middle Eastern sense. It is difficult to overemphasize the point. Most of us have been raised from childhood to think of God as a being infinitely distant from humanity or nature, and of the sacred as something separate from the profane. We have been taught that religion operates by different rules than politics, science, psychology, art, or culture. Yeshua's (Jesus') teaching and reported dealings with his followers show that he did not live from this type of separation thinking. Indeed, it should have been difficult for anyone at his time to entirely divorce Alaha (God) from the way that one related to one's community, to nature, or to the political forces of the time." (pp29,30)

We are Real within an "unreal world", but we do

not believe it because we accept the uninformed opinions of others rather than the Voice within us (We listen to **WEGO**). But the Sacred Voice within us (**WGOD**) quietly, gently, and confidently reassures that the Christ presence of Jesus is descriptive of an **identical** Christ Presence of Who We Are. What is there to fear? What is there to defend?

You'll say, "All of this is well and good, Westin, but have you tested it while you were pastor of a congregation?" "What is more important, how many parishioners could understand you?" Good questions! When I was ordained a Lutheran pastor in 1962, and preached my first sermons, there was little of the above emphasized.

In seminary, most everything written here was researched, and accepted by me. When we as newly trained pastors went out to our first parishes, we needed to close a tremendous gap separating us from the pre-Copernican biblical world-views still held by most parishioners. Remember, we had just finished concentrating on newer biblical understandings for a sustained four years in our "ivory towers." Did we share these?

I can't speak for my colleagues, but I now admit that I lacked the courage of my convictions. To share some of these ideas at my first church would have invited a visit from the Bishop. He would have advised that I was compromising my ordination vows, which required absolute adherence to the creeds and doctrines as interpreted by the church. With a family consisting of a loyal wife and four young sons, I was not going to jeopardize their security, especially having previously done so by leaving a law practice for the ministry.

Circumstances are such that the climate and demand by laity for higher critical biblical openness has changed considerably today. Bishop John Shelby Spong, whom I quote in both the introduction of this letter and the concluding chapter, shared with me that, "Our generation did try to keep critical biblical scholarship out of the life of our Churches. That was a pity." **This is why I urgently invite us today to get Real with the teachings of Jesus including who he was in history.**

The church has not, since the third and fourth centuries, experienced such a questioning of its "unity." That would include even the Reformation of the 16th century. Churches increasing their membership rolls today, for the most part, are those unquestioningly accepting the Bible literally as the "inerrant" Word of God. **Their interpretations are, in my opinion, at variance in several respects from the simpler and more picturesque Aramaic teachings of the *historic* Jesus of Nazareth.**

The church from which I recently retired, lovingly received the emphases of this letter over a period of 10 years. They are a community of aspiring followers of Jesus who taught us to *"Love one another **as** I have Loved you!"* There **is** a tremendous hunger for the Real teachings of Jesus, the Aramaic Middle Easterner. The people of Community Church of

Lauderdale-by-the Sea have been exposed to the interpretations of what is written here. *They and millions more are recognizing the difference between Jesus' teachings and the irrelevant doctrines of men.*

Bernard Brandon Scott and Robert W. Funk, known for their contributions to higher critical scholarship and, as *Fellows of the Jesus Seminar*, point out many of these differences. Please follow me carefully in the next few paragraphs and you can judge for yourselves the importance of getting Real with Jesus' teachings.

A few of the Aramaic words Jesus chose to describe God's activity among us were, "leaven" (yeast) and "mustard seed." In first century Palestine, these words had entirely different meanings from what many of us have been conveying to our congregations. Instead of leaven or mustard seeds symbolizing something positive, such as an expansive growth process within God's Kingdom or Realm, Jesus use of these terms actually caused his listeners to "perk up their ears." He was teaching something quite different from what they were accustomed to hear. He was literally "shaking them up." I quote from Scott's insightful book, *Re-Imagine the World*:

> **"Leaven is a symbol for moral evil,** the unclean; 'unleavened' bread more appropriately signifies the divine. At Passover "for seven days no leaven shall be found in your houses." (Exodus 12:19) . . . and twice Paul quotes the

aphorism "A little leaven leavens the whole lump" (Gal. 5:9; 1 Cor. 5:6.) The purpose of this aphorism is to warn that a little evil will corrupt everything. It parallels the American aphorism "One rotten apple spoils the whole barrel." And Jesus warns his disciples to "Beware of the leaven of the Pharisees." (Mark 8:15.) It is not too extreme to say that the juxtaposition of empire (Kingdom) of God and leaven is blasphemous. The comparison of the Empire of Rome to leaven would be more appropriate."

As for the mustard seed? It is only a weed-like noxious plant polluting the garden, making it *unclean*. From Mark's Gospel, let's read:

Again he said, "What shall we say the kingdom of God is like, or What parable shall we use to describe it? It is like a mustard seed, which is the smallest seed you plant in the ground. Yet when planted, It grows and becomes the largest of all garden plants, with such big branches that the birds of the air can perch in its shade." Mk 4:30-32.

If you were a Palestinian listener of the first century A.D., you would pick up your ears upon hearing Jesus mention "*big* branches" or "birds of the air nesting therein." What would more probably pop into your mind would be the much more majestic image of the noble cedar tree of Lebanon; not some noxious bit of garden shrubbery. So why does Jesus use the pathetic imagery of a garden weed? Scott concludes,

> "The answer is clear. An empire is more like a cedar of Lebanon. But Jesus' parable *burlesques* this assumption. It pokes fun at our expectation that an empire must be a mighty anything. Caesar's empire or Herod's client kingdom might have such pretensions. **But for Jesus, God's Empire is *more pervasive* than dominant.** It is like a pungent weed that takes over everything and in which the birds of the air can nest; It bears little if any resemblance to the mighty, majestic, and noble symbol of empire of Israel or Caesar. Take your choice, says the parable." (*Re-Imagine the World*, by Bernard Brandon Scott, p39)

Well, this contrasts radically with the way some have **misinterpreted Jesus' metaphorical teaching style,** as a Galilean peasant speaking Aramaic. He was really telling his listeners, God is on the side of the sick, the diseased, the powerless and defenseless because they are the ones who are in need of help. This is why Jesus spent most of his time in the company of "sinners, tax collectors, and prostitutes." **God 'inhabits' a world of the unclean and the diseased and the no-accounts.** Those who are "honorable," "righteous," and, beyond any need for improvement, "don't require God's guidance." Do you see the thrust of Jesus' teaching? (Who of us can say he is not sick? Were this so he wouldn't be living on planet Earth). Jesus was a Teacher par excellence! When he spoke, people listened. Some lives were significantly changed for the better. Jesus consistently ridiculed the hypocrisy of pious religious leaders!

"Unleavened" or "pure" empires that lord it over other kingdoms (as when Rome subjugated nations seeking their freedom and independence.) are *not* to be emulated! This was a *tongue-in-cheek* sort of emphasis. The people of Jesus' day clearly understood what he meant. Jesus was an Eastern-Mediterranean Teacher who communicated brilliantly, even cynically, through the picture language of Aramaic. Rome recognized the threat he represented and executed Jesus accordingly. These are but a few examples then of how Jesus' teachings have been misinterpreted and, consequently, distorted and watered down. I again reiterate, **"Let's get Real with Jesus' teachings!"**

Is it not time we understand how and why Jesus of Nazareth was a 'threat' to the established governments and prevailing religious leadership of his day? (Perhaps we can see this even with reference to today's world crises?) Bernard Brandon Scott pulls no punches as he summarizes what we have written:

> "The reason(s) for the death of Jesus probably remain beyond our grasp. . . . Pilate did not really need a solid case to kill Jesus. Yet one can see in Jesus' *language-activity* the seeds of a conflict that could easily escalate to a confrontation and

to death . . . For Empire is built on the premise that the local populations are divided and distrustful of each other. A peasantry who accept each other, who no longer see themselves competing with each other . . . even reaching out to Samaritan enemies — such a peasantry poses a real threat to Rome's rule by thwarting its attempts to divide and conquer."

Not much has changed in these past 2000 years. Having lived with political assassinations throughout the 60's to date, we should be able to appreciate current events. A follower of Jesus of Nazareth, the Galilean peasant, who chooses today to get Real can expect similar treatment. Perhaps not in our country today you say? Remember, Gandhi, Martin Luther King Jr., and Dietrich Bonhoffer? (The Lutheran Pastor hanged by Hitler in 1945 before the Allies entered Berlin.) These were men who valued God's ways ahead of popular opinion. Read Bonhoffer's, *The Cost of Discipleship* or King's, *Letters From A Birmingham Prison*. **You will readily understand why the practice of unconditional Love and Peace is threatening to the entrenched interests of rulers and other authority figures.**

Nevertheless, Whenever we participate from within a Perception of Love that is inclusive of all of Creation, there Really can be no "death, evil, sin, nor injustice" to fear. **For those able to accept that there is no opposite to Love,** such compelling conviction explains why and how the world's great spiritual leaders lived lives of fearless Love and

Peace **for** all of us. "I have seen the Mountain" or "I have a dream," words spoken by Martin Luther King Jr. shortly before he was killed, tell me that he lived simultaneously in two complementary worlds; each one supportive of the other. What's to fear!

I conclude this chapter with another example of how differently Reality is viewed among those of us in the West from our brothers who live in the Eastern Hemisphere. Compare, if you will, the familiar John 3:16 in both Aramaic and English translations:

> "For Unity so loved Diversity, all the worlds of form, that it brought you a child of Unity, fulfilled in all aspects of self, so that whoever would have the same confidence in their own fulfillment, like the earth underneath supporting all, would not fade with their form, but continue, from world to world, with and in the ever-living Life." (The Hidden Gospel, pg.123)

> "For God so loved the world, that he gave his only begotten Son, That whosover believeth in him should not perish, but have ever- lasting life." (John 3:16, KJV)

CHAPTER FIVE

LEVEL CONFUSION

I CANNOT CONCEIVE of nor believe that God has a split personality. The Creator cannot be both hateful and loving. Any god who justifies war and the killing of innocent and "guilty" people, is not the Abba/Daddy of Jesus' affections. I refuse to believe in a 'dualistic' deity; nor did Jesus. Had he, then he could not have taught us to *"Love your enemies and do good to those who harm you."* Such beliefs have led towards too much unnecessary confusion among those who have formulated their doctrines about God.

There is a marvelous resource upon which I rely in my thinking and experiencing **Love**. It is *A COURSE IN MIRACLES*. I have been a student and teacher of the Course since 1986. The course has much to say about why we are confused. It's appropriately a "study course" since it consists of a text, workbook, and manual for teachers. The author, in my opinion, is Jesus of Nazareth, the Galilean peasant, teacher, and healer.

Some critics would say, derisively, "it is channeled" and then, dismiss it summarily as "New Age." But, think about it, how do you suppose any inspirational writings or compositions materialize? Are we prone to think these originate only from within the level of our egos? Of course not! Religious people **themselves** acknowledge a most Omnipotent Channel called Holy Spirit. This is but an obvious example of level confusion. A channel, according to the dictionary, is a course or passage through which something may be moved or directed. (ex. a channel of thought). From where do our thoughts originate?

When I experience the music of a great violinist or pianist, I see and/or hear the composer's musical thought being performed or channeled through the musician. Handel's Oratorio, *the Messiah*, or Beethoven's *Ode to Joy* are frequently channeled by gifted people. Oftentimes while preaching, I have experienced the feeling of being a channel of Love's extensions. This occurs especially when delivering a sermon or a speech without notes. Being "in-Spired" or *in the Spirit* would be another way of saying this. "Did that come out of my mouth?" is frequently my reaction. I quoted the following earlier from the Introduction to the Course: *NOTHING REAL CAN BE THREATENED. NOTHING UNREAL EXISTS. HEREIN LIES THE PEACE OF GOD*. There are nearly 1,500,000 copies of the Course circulating throughout the world and it has been translated into eight different languages.

(Incidentally, I will be eternally grateful to a lady in my congregation, in 1986, who introduced me to the Course.) The above statement has clarified 'level confusion' for me.

During our daily pursuits, there are numerous occasions when we act and react from different levels of awareness. We don't pay attention to this. Perhaps we should. For example, in the following experience someone might ask, "What kind of lawyer are you, Howard, if you resort to channeled information to persuade us about the historical Jesus of Nazareth as your Teacher?" As a criminal defense attorney, I admit to some unusual, if not inexplicable "arguments" bordering on level confusion. Like a murder case I defended successfully in Toledo, Ohio. Afterwards, while sharing a drink with the prosecuting attorney, he chided me and said, "You violated just about every one of the Rules of Criminal Procedure, it's a miracle you were able to pull it off!" I know he was right but I didn't intentionally circumvent procedural law. I did what a deep intuitive feel of the moment led me to do. (Excuse me Judge, I was channeling from another level!)

People ask why I gave up the practice of law to become a minister. The only answer I could give or sing is like the experience referenced in the ballad "Blowin in the Wind." You knew I was going to say . . ." I heard a very gentle Voice within inviting me to try a different road." On every path you and I take throughout Life there are many forks (channels.) As the Course teaches, **"We are on a journey without**

distance." Maybe that statement confuses you? It won't if the level you choose is that of Beingness or Spirit or Peace or Love. There are no time and space limitations within the level of Love. From within your own Identity, you **do know** the qualitative difference between the mundane and the Holy! **You just Know!** A time arrives when you prefer roast beef to spam.When I began Law school in the 50's, I was introduced to the 'case-book' method of instruction. Our professors would challenge us to get to the issues and define these concisely. We would brief each case, standing before our peers, being prepared to defend either the plaintiff's or defendant's positions. The holdings of all courts and reasons for their rulings were included in the exercises. Gullibility or naivetes were inexcusable. Our arguments were adversarial. Take sides, any side, and be prepared to reason clearly.

The reason for this slight detour was to assure you I still retain a lawyer's mind. Of much more importance, I have uncovered within me a latent Christ-Mind. Confusing? Remember my understanding of the Christ as God Presence and/or Holy Spirit? This is the same as, in a Holy Instant, hearing, recognizing, and enjoying the Real Counselor's Voice! If we learn how to be still when we arrive at our own confusing, troublesome, and puzzling forks in the road, signposts **do light up** pointing to the correct channel or voice. I do recognize, however, that there can be considerable static-confusion interfering with which voice we hear!

I do not like confrontation! That is another reason for no longer practicing law. My mind is gradually being weaned away from adversarial or *dualistic* thinking. "What are you saying here, Howie?" Well, everything I've written so far acknowledges that most of us think and live from within a world of opposites: Good and Bad; Right and Wrong; Black and White; Male and Female; Rich and Poor; Young and Old. We live in a dualistic world. Jesus taught otherwise. If we are *In this world but really not of it*, then, **of which world are we?** From which level are we thinking, doing, Creating?

Jesus taught about **Beingness existing Now,** in what he called the Kingdom of Heaven, informing us, in effect, **there are no opposites.** He, himself, lived life that way. "Orthodox" Christianity with its creeds, doctrines, and biblical interpretations resembles the State and its varied documents of governance. Indeed, the model, particularly for the Roman Catholic Church, has been the Roman Empire. My point is that Church and State, alike, are *dualistic systems.* Inevitably each of them, **being politically adversarial,** add to the confusion of who is right or wrong; conservative or liberal etc. Level confusion occurs whenever people converse from different perceptions about the same issues. Like the proverbial "ships passing in the night," they are not aware of the route or "channel" each is traveling. A scholar and a mystic sit down to discuss a passage of scripture. The scholar, on the level of logic and reason, attempts to explain the Doctrine of the Trinity; while the mystic experiences the Presence of God as ineffable and awesome. Both are right; but each is in a different channel. They may or may not be in agreement. **That is level confusion.**

This letter I am writing is, on one level, an attempt to rationally explain my beliefs about Love and Peace. It is, on another level, a sharing of my **experiencing** of Love and Peace. The difference is like reading the classified ads, and then suddenly, as though out of nowhere, experiencing beautiful, peaceful feelings of Love and Compassion. **We can, in a timeless moment, channel these from the depths of our Beingness.** That is when time stands still, being experienced as a "journey without distance," with words no longer needed to express the awesome Presence of Love.

We live in a Global Age where "East is West, and North is South." Sound confusing? You and I are our "brother's keeper" and together we need all become peacemakers, not adversaries. How many millions more need be killed? This world is in need of a newer perspective; a **Truer Perception**. Perhaps, **you** will write your letters and shout from the rooftops how you are seeing things differently. It may be from the perspective of Jesus of Nazareth, the Galilean. Or, your Path might be that of the Buddha, or Mohammed, the Prophet. Your beliefs may be humanistic or atheistic; it matters not as much as knowing **Who You Really Are!** Labels are unimportant. **Doing Love IS The Real living of Your Life! No confusing this!**

Being and Doing are inseparable; and so we are, you and me. We can do IT together NOW! We **can** Love one another if we choose. Another mantra/ affirmation I repeat several times a day is, *"I Love You Father with all of my heart; soul; mind; and strength and my neighbor as myself. I Love myself* *unconditionally; I heal myself completely. I teach others Love; I teach others healing. Happiness prevails and pervades every event of my life and I share that happiness with every one I meet."*

What is your affirmation? Who is your channel? Whatever you choose is manifested in this world. You are that **powerful** according to all the sages! You can "Move mountains!" You can promote and manifest Peace among the nations and people!

CHAPTER SIX

REALISTS AND DREAMERS

"YOU ARE A dreamer, Westin, and what you are writing is impractical. Justice requires the criminal be punished and terrorists hunted down and put to death. If what you tell us is actually what your historical Jesus preached and taught 2000 years ago then both of you are crazy!" May I borrow a phrase from one of our former presidents? "Let me make one thing perfectly clear" I am indeed a pacifist. Until my last breath, I will argue that war never solved the problems of our planet. As this is being written, it appears inevitable that we will go to war again.

Always, we promise that each war is in order to prevent future wars and unless we, America, have a strong Defense then the free world is in peril. Free, I might add, according to our belief that we, the most powerful nation in the world, are true guardians of peace. Ironically, we have named one of our ballistic missiles

"The Peacemaker." However we flex our military muscles, as on a Russian May Day celebration in Red Square, or display to the world our superior Air Force, Navy, Army, and Marine Corps, when the dust lifts some decades hence, what will we have left that is any different from the ashes of the Third Reich or the Roman Empire? A friend of mine, when asked if the day would come when we no longer had wars replied, "Not so long as two men are standing." I do not agree. I could not write this letter if I believed this.

Jesus and his followers are the true Realists. I believe that the world and its constituted governments and leaders are themselves dreamers. Jesus said, taught, and lived, *"Give to Caesar what belongs to Caesar but to God what belongs to God."* Our politicians and leaders are not going to change the world for us. We're going to have to do that ourselves. In the same way, the church is not your 'savior;' *you Are*! **I am a pacifist and a 'Realist' and, I boldly assert, an optimist, too.** Who are you?

The historical Jesus of Nazareth was an extraordinary Healer. So are millions of this world's citizens! Whether they are home exercising and jogging and walking or shopping at the health food stores, today's populace is much farther ahead of previous generations in their willingness to improve in the care of body and mind. This is a bit paradoxical since we are a nation with the worst obesity problem in the world.

Nevertheless, visit a health spa or a gym, you will see a gigantic leap in health consciousness from the

50's and the 60's when your local YMCA's and YWCA's were the only outlets. Fly over this great nation at night and recognize as you cross over our cities and towns the number of playgrounds, tennis courts, and baseball diamonds teeming with people intent on physical exercise and refreshing re-creation of their spirits.

Read the expanded coverage of sports events and view on television those world events where athletes, for the most part, respect and salute each other. A world telecast from Japan during the opening ceremonies of the winter Olympics simulcast to every continent Beethoven's *Ode to Joy*. This was sung simultaneously throughout the world **at and in** the very Precious Moment of a Present NOW! None of us will ever forget September 11, 2001, as an entire world mourned a devastating loss of life, touching every household with sorrow. And again, what sadness was occasioned by the recent loss of the *"Columbia"* and its heroic crew. Yet, many hearts are continually revitalized by Hope as together we evolve into a world of increasing compassionate caring. This is **Love frequenting every** saddened doorstep and this is **Love** as it is *Really* experienced. It is not a dream. No way!

Many are also improving their spiritual understanding. Every large community features frequent workshops on Spirituality. People representing every age group attend, and, judging by the crowds, these are as popular as a Rock and

Roll Concert featuring the latest stars and attractions. I, indeed, am an optimist.

I cheerfully, enthusiastically, endorse the cry "We're Number One" with the understanding that there are no exclusions. **Oneness includes each and every One of us!** That is the world we are becoming as Berlin walls and, ultimately, separation walls among people come tumbling down stone by stone. We are doing it together and becoming One. Earth's **homo sapiens, a wiser humanity,** is gradually advancing along a path of Global healing and Peace. Literally, hundreds of thousands march for world peace even as this is being written (January, 2003). They abhor the nightmare of waging another war that cannot, nor ever will produce the Oneness of Humanity. They are the salt of the Earth!

Look at what is progressively happening within the medical community. Revolutionary! Apart from all the problems inherent in a lack of universal medical benefits affordable to all, there has been the expansion and public acceptance of alternative procedures resulting in effective and amazing results. Thanks to people like Brian Weiss, Deepak Chopra, Wayne Dyer, Larry Dossey, Dr. Phil and his good friend, Oprah, people are opening up to new possibilities of healing. And, were there to be only one statement on healing attributable to Jesus, it has to be *"Heal thyself, pick up your mat and walk.*" **Do it and quit feeling sorry for yourself.** There's an expert Healer within you.All of the above takes effort. No one worth his salt is going to change without exerting tremendous, persistent, willingness to become the very best. Actually, carrying out a conscious resolution to change requires a lot of courage. You and I, at our deepest levels of existence, encounter a strong resistance within our unconscious minds in dealing with deeply rooted beliefs and prejudices.

Growth appears to be a slow process. The mighty oak tree has a lengthy history beginning with its origin as an acorn. And yes, I certainly understand the meaning of teaching "an old dog" new tricks. Remember, it has taken me seven decades to begin the practice of what I preach. I'm working on being Real, gradually awakening from dreams. Just think, Jesus was about thirty-two and fully awake when he "died". That is why he is the most memorable and esteemed human being within recorded history!

Ask yourself these questions, "What is my purpose for living on planet Earth?" or "Why am I here?" and, "Am I really that important to the universe?" Then listen to the approval of a Benevolent Creator saying, *"My dear Daughter (Son), in you I am well pleased."* Our Self respect need not be earned so far as God is concerned; for we are marvelously Created as a Work of Art — El Perfecto! Great news to believe, right?

We Are a unique Thought of God! We will not believe this while our attention is centered on our egos, and *that is not who we are!* We retain a blurred self-image of ourselves; certainly not that perfect Image of God, the Bible tells us we Are. External feed-back is what we continually seek. "Mirror,

mirror, on the wall, who's the fairest of us all?" The advertising industry could not exist were we as certain as God how perfect and beautiful We Are. Why not choose Real Life instead of dreaming dreams?

Take a meaningful trip! Instead of escaping through misuse of drugs and, blowing your mind, go inside, deeply inside your Self. Do this regularly for twenty minutes twice a day, and resonate with the music of heaven "Blowin' in the Wind" of your own sacred breath. In fact, practice breathing deeply for several minutes, and see how much sooner you arrive fully conscious in a peaceful state of restfulness. There you can hear station **WGOD. Allow your body, mind, and Spirit to merge in the Oneness of Love's Peaceful energy and you will experience the difference between dreams and Reality.**

I repeat often each day. *"I am not a body. I am free. For I am still as God created me."* (ACIM 2nd Ed W.201,pg 388) As I learn to accept the high regard with which our Creator views us, I am free to *Be* in what each moment presents, and **Love as "She" Loves**. These past two chapters have been intended as encouragement for us to see things differently. "Letting go and letting God" is an option of our wills to **Be as God Created Us:** to live Life courageously as have countless thousands throughout the history of humanity . . . **getting Real with the teachings of the Real Jesus.**

Samuel Taylor Coleridge wrote these relevant and provocative words:

"What if you slept? And what if, in your sleep, you dreamed? And what if, in your dream, you went to heaven and there plucked a beautiful flower? And what if, when you awoke, You had the flower in your hand? Ah, what then?"

CHAPTER SEVEN

THE POWER OF 'I AM'

I HEARD A famous actress say, "It is much easier to be happy than depressed." She was right. You and I know many people who, despite their physical and mental challenges, are genuinely happy. I remember several visits to a Home for mentally challenged children where, upon the arrival of visitors, these "Honest to God" kids would surround us with mirthful laughter and welcoming smiles. No pretensions; just unconditional acceptance.

During a visit to Haiti, there is etched in my mind an unforgettable scene. The poorest of the poor live in circumstances worse than swine. Hundreds of thousands of our brothers and sisters are forced to survive under conditions unimaginable to us. Nor are they able to immigrate to other nations without being separated from other seekers of freedom and shipped back or held in quarantined compounds.

Standing on a dung heap which happened to be higher ground, a young girl put her hand in mine and, in broken English said, "You my friend." Her swollen belly indicated she was suffering from extreme malnutrition having but a few months left to live. She wasn't crying. Her face radiated with the warmest smile I've ever seen. She taught me how **Powerful a Presence** there was within us. I was in the presence of "**I AM.**" Am I not continually grateful to her and is she not one of my favorite Teachers? And did not our Jewish brother say that "*Unless we become **as** these children*" we will not experience the happiness and peace they Know?

I recall Jesus saying, "*The birds of the heavens have no anxiety and the flowers of the field are more beautifully attired than King Solomon*" and that, in effect, we lack nothing. We own it all together because **we and "I AM" are One.** The "property ownership" deed recorded in the Universe lists our names as Grantees in absolute fee simple. (Sorry, I can't resist using some lawyer language.) Each and every one of the billions of us inhabiting planet Earth are Co-Owners, together with a most generous Grantor-Creator! Unbelievable! **His many mansions belong to all of us.** The title to that deed could read, **from I AM to I AM.**

"Oh, you are a dreamer, Westin." Yes, I am. The ditty, "Row, row, row your boat, gently down the stream; merrily, merrily, merrily, merrily, life is but a dream," could apply here. All of us **are** dreamers especially if we think Life begins and ends merely with physical existence. Where have we been while the quantum physicists tell us that what appears as solid physical matter can, and does eventually, transmute back into formless energy? And that *there is no time and space in the absolute sense!* **Just think, the Scientists and Biblical scholars, as well as the Mystics, are speaking the same language.** They are in agreement that we are all *interconnected.*I joyfully share the following dream-experience I had several years ago. Early in the morning before waking, I had, what some may call an 'out-of-body' experience; an extraordinary vision. Before me was an endless universe containing billions upon trillions of stars. I just Knew, instantly, that each and every one of the stars (or Beings) were cognizant of one another and they were communicating intelligently and simultaneously with each other within a **timelessness of NOWNESS**. And then . . . I was aware of a Voice saying, **"What you see I AM"**. (If you require a Name for Creation Itself, I don't believe you could improve on **I AM.**)

Shakespeare said something similar when he wrote "To be or not to be, that is the question." As a child, I have had experiences of Peacefulness tingle in every nerve fiber of my body. These feelings arose whenever my consciousness seemingly was being addressed. In later years I accepted this as a Presence of the *I AM or Christ-Self.* More and more people are *admitting* they too have experienced this. This is terrific news is it not? Many already are publicizing these remarkable experiences via sattelites and wireless telephones and the Internet. We are becoming more willing to declare our Real Identities as I AM.

Smiling and being happy **is** our natural state. We need not work at being happy. It is not a matter of putting on a happy face or covering up the frown lines with makeup. The actress we quoted at the beginning of this chapter added, "You've got to work at being depressed." Somewhat like a clown painting a sad appearance over his naturally happy face. The sadness is real only for the duration of the make-up; Happiness just **IS**. But then, you may ask, "Why are there increasingly so many more depressed people?"

Read Eckhart Tolle's *The Power of Now.* Out of a transforming spiritual experience, Tolle had learned, at age 29, to dissolve an old identity mired in sadness. He then proceeded to rediscover a Presence within himself, transmuting all past guilt and future fear. Over the years, Tolle cultivated the art of living without having to mask his true Self. He took note of the unconscious undercurrents of unease affecting him. As an observer of this unease, he learned to suspend any negative stuff making-up his wrong-mindedness. Translation: we think wrongfully too much of the time! Digging up the past and allowing it to paralyze the present with what no longer is, virtually blinds us to what **IS Now**. The past cannot hurt us, unless we allow it to become real. That is a matter of thinking it so, is it not? As we evolve, we will eventually realize how thinking, of itself, is only a minor aspect of an **Infinite Field of Consciousness** within **the Realm of Beingness**. There is where we truly Live. Give those last thoughts some deep consideration please. As some of the ancients put it, *In Him we live and move and have our Being.* (That's **present** tense, folks.)

Jesus observed that most of us *do not really see with our eyes nor hear with our ears.* Real Knowledge, as previously defined, is *veiled* from our hearts. Instead of listening and envisioning *consciously,* to what some call an abiding Christ Presence, we identify with countless external noises and distractions. We think about tomorrow neglecting what is before us this instant. In that state of mind of living in the past, how can we be *presently* Alive? You only Live in the Eternal Present. The past and the future are manufactured by a non-existing ego. "It" intrudes upon, as well as crowds out, the Creative Present. When we truly see what is directly in front of us, and actually hear what someone is saying, we co-Create and Do and Be. This occurs whenever the Creator's Will is done on Earth *as* it is in Heaven.

You are the Teacher. You are the Healer. You are, as Jesus reminded his disciples, Servers of Tender Loving Care. So, when you become sad and depressed, go to a retirement home and cheer these lonely people with your happy face. Is not that what celebrities and famous athletes do in their spare time? Just keep doing it all the time in elevators or standing in line at the super market or bank, you hear? Guess what? This kind of practice results in your consciously choosing much more often a Way of Living Life meshing with the Will of our Creator. It could become a habit you would gladly choose regularly. It is the Answer for you Now. **Try It, you'll Love It!**

There is a tradition that Abraham Lincoln said,

"God must have loved the common people because he created so many of them." On planet Earth live about seven billion common people. I believe several millions **Do** all of the above because they have awakened to their Beingness. With governments gradually becoming more democratized and less dictatorial, the people of this world are choosing to elect more and more of their own. The day will yet be celebrated when a majority of planet Earth's leaders, with the rest of the common people, will learn war no more.

Nevertheless, whether or not this planet survives our mismanagement, it will eventually disappear and be transformed into some other awesome aspect of the Infinite energy Field of Love; the Fabric of Beingness, or Creation. **What is virtually, ultimately Real, is Love.** The marvel of Creation is this continuum of Love's extension within people, souls, planets, stars, atoms, etc. It is beyond our current intelligence. Truly, it has been said, "Only God Knows!" Our coinage has the motto: "In God We Trust." Do we really trust God? If we do, what are we waiting for? We can move mountains with millions of us voting Yes for Love and No to fear. As Franklin Delano Roosevelt said during the critical years of the 30's, "The only thing we have to fear is fear itself."

God's identity as revealed to Moses is simply defined: **I AM THAT I AM.** This Is a God without a face of any color or gender, a God appearing in fire and light and earth and wind. He is not only the I AM of you and me; **He Is God for the whole of Creation!** Seyyed Hossein Nasr, Professor of Islamic

Studies, at George Washington University in Washington, D.C. wrote,

> "Today, however, those who speak of God, and at the same time have concern for humanity, **must also address themselves to God's Creation.** It is necessary to protect nature not on the basis of mere sentimentality but on the firm ground of the knowledge of God both in himself and in his manifestations . . . . Approaching God requires of us that we seek the light that both illuminates and enlivens: the sun that is the source of liberating knowledge and the warmth that is the love that flows throughout the universe and gives life to all things. **This is the light that will allow us to see the divine** presence everywhere and to hear the voice of the sacred not only in the *B Minor Mass of Bach but also in the song of birds, the chant of whales, and the thunderous sound of storms.*" (Underlining and darkening mine.)

We *are* the Reflections of God. We *are* God's Manifestations of Love *within* planet Earth. In other words, **you and I are "I AM!"** One with the Creator? Awesome!

CHAPTER EIGHT

UNDOING THE MISTAKES

THE YEAR WAS 1946. I'd arrived in Germany en route to Austria where I served in the Army Air Corps as a weather observer. A very youthful eighteen, I observed much more than the weather. Upon disembarking from our aircraft in Frankfurt, a DP, (displaced person) lifted my duffle bag upon his shoulder and, as I followed him to the ground transportation area, a young girl of about eight or nine appeared at my side. In German, she said, "schlaufen mit meine schwester, zwei cigarretten bitteschoen."

Translation: "Sleep with my sister for two cigarettes." Surrounding me was the stench and rubble of destroyed buildings as people were shoveling and cleaning up the debris. By the time my tour of duty was over, in late 1948, the Marshall Plan, (A United States program of assistance to countries of war-torn Europe), had enabled the

German people to rebuild their cities considerably. What does this say to you? My take on it is that war is hell; war is a tragic mis-take of humanity.

In spite of this, I believe that underlying the grief, pain, and suffering each of us experiences, **a greater good can undo the worst of conditions**. This greater good is **Love**. We eventually confront the darkness of our souls, pick up our mats, and rise from the ashes of a despondent despair like the proverbial Phoenix. How does that happen? **There is resilience to our Spirits**. Within our consciousness a Voice is heard; a Voice previously muted by the incessant wrong-minded chatter of the ego.

Jesus, in his *Parable of the Prodigal Son*, paints a masterful picture for us. After the prodigal son comes to his senses, choosing to undo his mis-takes and return home to his father, he rediscovers Love Itself (his father) had really never left him. The elder brother (ourselves?) had yet to learn this lesson! The story is found in the *Gospel of Luke* (Chapter 15) and illustrates Jesus' trust in a Creator/Father/Abba-Daddy Who leads each of us out from behind the shadows of despondency. (Similar to the 23rd Psalm, relating how the Shepherd leads his sheep into greener pastures.)

Another scene reminiscent of the "Dark night of the Soul" takes place in the garden of Gethsemane. Jesus, alone in prayer, and aware of his imminent physical death, asks to be spared. With the resilience of Spirit within him, he trustingly says, *"Not my will but Yours be done."* So much as to say, **"Your Love Father**

will suffice to see me through this." Any member of AA knows something about how another's Love enables him to undo a path of self destruction. Nor could I write this letter had I not experienced these dark nights many times only to rise up again.

Any situation where you and another person are unable to communicate, poses a disruption to the *unity of all humanity*. None of us lives our life apart from others. What affects you affects me. Disagreements of a hostile and abusive nature constantly arise rearing their ugly heads; frequently with people 'squaring off' and hurling slanderous verbal missiles. My Teacher once said that anyone who hates his brother is, in fact, a "murderer." Hating and cursing others may not seem to be on the same level as physical violence, but the end result is the same. A relationship has been *severed*. It awaits restoration, forgiveness, and undoing. Like Sinatra singing, "Regrets, I've had a few," so we have committed our many *mis-takes* which await correction.

Until the conscious will and desire to forgive becomes ingrained within us, we will continually behave insanely and, as the Mills Brothers tune has it, "only hurt the one we love." **Forgiveness is letting go.** Completely! Ask yourself whenever you are about to do battle, "Would I rather be right or happy?" Observe what happens when you button your lips and respond with a calm demeanor. Either the other party will keep on jabbering for a while and finally walk away pouting, or, with a surprised expression of disbelief, open the door and join with you in a resumption of civility.

The repeated and daily practice of blinding one's self to the faults of others is very rewarding. *"Judge not,"* Jesus said, *"And you will not be judged."* Do not make real what has no Reality. Don't lay guilt trips on others or yourself. These are the positive exercises we can implement immediately and gradually see things differently. Also, eliminate that word "sin." Its true meaning has been distorted in its translation from the Greek language.

The original connotation for sin meant 'to *miss* the mark'; like failing to hit a target with an arrow. We are not wretched sinners awaiting the dreaded Last Judgment. We make *mis*-takes. Countless *mis*-takes. **Mis-takes can be corrected while sins are condemnatory**. A Hollywood director orders a retake of a scene he is filming. Take one . . . take seven, whatever the number, and these takes are only ***mis*-takes!** *A Course in Miracles* is helpful in understanding what we are discussing. Orthodox Christianity teaches many theories on how "sin" is forgiven. These are called atonement theories. Some bear striking resemblances to primitive beliefs about appeasing angry and offended gods. The term "sin-offering," mentioned in the Bible, refers to a ritual performed by ancient priests. They would gather their congregations around an altar upon which an unblemished lamb would be slain. The lamb represented the sinful people who were being spared from the wrath of the gods. So that the people wouldn't forget their wrongful acts, the priests, with ladles of warm animal blood scooped from the troughs, splashed the people as a reminder of the mercy the gods have shown.

That brutal ritual of sacrifice is illegal due to recent laws enacted by state legislatures. Why, then, is it still an integral part of liturgical-atonement practices within church worship? The answer? God is yet viewed by many as wrathful and in need of appeasement. That is insane. Such a weak god! Who of us, listening to Jesus' teachings about Abba, choose to worship a god entirely opposite and alien to Jesus' experiences of Our Father? As the Course reminds us, the world we have made is topsy-turvy from Creation Itself. We **can** choose to see the world differently. Thanks to Jesus' teachings about a Loving Creator, we can get a glimpse now of **Creation as It Really Is!**

Atonement, from the Course perspective means we can, under the guidance of Spirit, **undo** our **mis-takes**. St. Paul had it right when he said, *"I can do all things in and through Christ Who strengthens me."* If we can do, we can also undo. The Bible is a mixed bag. There are many truthful teachings to be found there. There are also included the thoughts and false interpretations of men. You and I do have the ability to respond to our *mis*-takes and correct them. By the way, the definition of the word responsibility is: "having the ability to respond." We need no other Co-Responder than the Holy Spirit, our Counselor. "It" enables us to Do and Act and Co-Create! "She" is our Correspondent.

There is a beautiful teaching about God's assisting "Grace to us" in the Course. I repeat it daily as part of the **"undoing"** of my many **mis-takes:**

> *"It is a new and holy day today, for we receive what has been given us. Our faith lies in the Giver, not our own acceptance. We acknowledge Our mistakes, but He to Whom all error is unknown is yet the One Who answers our mistakes by giving us the means to lay them down, and rise to Him in gratitude and love. And He descends to meet us, as we come to Him." (W pl 168.5:2)*

A humorous incident took place during worship at Community Church. An elder presented me with a sign while I was making some announcements. This read, "Always, always, always listen to Annie." Annie, my dear wife, continually reminds me of this daily as I continually make my *mis*-takes and fail, sometimes intentionally, to listen to her. There is a related sign in my mind: **"Always, always, always listen to the Holy Spirit."**

CHAPTER NINE

1,500,000,000 POTENTIAL STORY TELLERS

I LOVE READING books! Before purchasing the laptop computer on which this letter is being typed, I procrastinated; buying and reading a couple dozen more books for inspiration. There are so many excellent authors out there.

Among the writers I admire greatly, is Alan Cohen, best selling author of *The Dragon Doesn't Live Here Anymore*. Alan has a flair for telling stories one of which I want to share with you. It provides a delightful comparison to the last chapter.

"Once upon a time, in a tropical land there lived a king who had an advisor. This lieutenant was so positive, in fact, that the king was often annoyed by his practice of constantly finding good in everything.

One day, while the king and the lieutenant were on a journey through the jungle, the king was chopping a fresh coconut for breakfast, and his machete slipped, cutting off his toe. The aching monarch limped to show his misfortune to the lieutenant, who exclaimed, "That's wonderful!"

"What did you say?" Asked the king, astonished.

"This is a real blessing!"

Hearing this response, the king became very angry; this man was obviously poking fun at his mishap.

"Take it from me," the lieutenant exhorted, "behind this apparent accident there is some good we do not see."

That was the last straw! Furious, the king picked up the lieutenant and hurled him into a dry well. Then he set out to find his way back to his castle.

En route, the potentate was apprehended by a band of headhunters who decided that he would make an excellent sacrifice for this month's offering to the volcano. The warriors took him to the tribal priest, who prepared him for the dubious honor.

As the holy man was anointing the reluctant sacrifice, he noticed that the king was missing a toe. "I'm sorry," the priest informed the king, "we can't use you. The volcano goddess accepts only full-bodied sacrifices; you are free to go."

Overjoyed, the king hobbled out of the tribal camp. Suddenly, it dawned on him that the lieutenant had been correct—there was, indeed, a blessing behind this seeming misfortune!

As quickly as he could, the king found his way back to the well where he had left the lieutenant. To the ruler's delight, his companion was still sitting in the well, whistling happily. (He was, indeed, a positive thinker!) The king offered the lieutenant a hand, pulled him out of the well, and apologized profusely.

"I am terribly sorry I threw you in there!" the king confessed, as he dusted his advisor's shoulders. "I was taken prisoner by some wild natives who were about to cast me into the volcano. But when they saw my toe was missing, they let me go. It was actually a miracle, which you foretold—and I so thoughtlessly cast you into this pit! Can you ever forgive me?"

"No apology necessary," replied the

lieutenant. "It was also a blessing that you left me in the well."

"Now how are you going to make something positive out of that?" queried the king.

"Because," the lieutenant explained, "if I was with you, they would have taken me for the sacrifice!"

Jesus of Nazareth could have told that story! Think of it, the world of today is being taught and entertained by thousands of great artists, musicians, comedians, actors and actresses, speakers, and writers. Just realize our good fortune to have all these resourceful teachers. Think also of the movies, plays, musicals, and operas that inspire and educate.

The Internet circulates some of the greatest teachings imaginable. A friend forwarded one such familiar story I wish to share. Entitled *Unconditional Acceptance* it relates the true story of a mother of three recently completing college.

"The last class I had was Sociology. The teacher was absolutely inspiring with qualities that I wish every human being had been graced with. Her last project of the term was called "Smile," The class was asked to go out and smile at three people and document their reactions. I am a very friendly person and always smile at everyone and say hello anyway, so, I thought this would be a piece of cake, literally."

"Soon after we were assigned the project, my husband, youngest son, and I went out to McDonald's one crisp March morning. We were standing in line, waiting to be served, when all of a sudden everyone around us began to back away. An overwhelming feeling of panic welled up inside of me as I turned to see why they had moved. As I turned around, I smelled a horribly dirty body odor, and there standing behind me were two poor homeless men.

As I looked down at the shorter gentleman close to me, he was smiling. His beautiful sky blue eyes were full of God's Light as he searched for acceptance. He said, "Good day," as he counted the few coins he had been clutching. The second man fumbled with his hands as he stood behind his friend. I realized he was mentally challenged.

"The young lady at the counter asked him what they wanted. He said,

"Coffee is all Miss," because that is all they could afford and, obviously, the only way they could sit inside a warm restaurant. Then I felt it. The compassion was so great I almost embraced the little man with the blue eyes. (I also noticed the other people watching me.)

"Smiling, I ordered two extra breakfast meals and walked over to the men with the tray, unable to resist touching the blue-eyed gentleman's cold hand. He looked up at me, with tears in his eyes, and said, "Thank you."

As I walked away to join my family, my husband smiled and said, "That is why God gave you to me, Honey, *to give me hope.*" I also realized then *that we as human beings, and being part of God, share this need to be healed and to heal people.* (Italics mine)

Jesus walked miles from village to village, healing the sick, telling stories from his first hand experiences of the Father's Realm. Most of his teachings were 'one-liners' or aphorisms. He didn't waste words. With parables and/or allegories, which he told masterfully, the faces of his listeners lit up with smiles! Jesus' stories were like diamonds whose facets emitted prisms of multicolored light! It hardly mattered whether you were well educated or illiterate, there was enough for everyone to think about. The people went out to him in droves as the word circulated from town to town about this Teacher and Healer who acted from *an authority of his own.*

What did he teach? Only Love!.

I have a 2'x4' color print which is a picture-parable. It shows Jesus sitting in a pew with his head resting on the shoulder of a man who, together with every one else in the congregation, appears oblivious to the 'robed' Jewish guest. The preacher is seen in the foreground with arms uplifted delivering his homily and not a single person is looking at him, nor Jesus. As for Jesus, he is asleep with a copy of the Village Voice on his lap. "So, when are you going to get with it?" That's the message I see in this poignant print. When are more and more of the 1,500,000,000 'nominal' Christians on planet Earth going to communicate the same challenging teachings as did Jesus 2,000 years ago?

I believe we should never teach children what later they must unlearn. The world about which children learn today is a world described by modern science. On the other hand, much of today's church-language about Jesus and the Bible perpetuates an **antiquated physical world-view which is no longer relevant.** Therefore, many stories in the Bible make no sense to children who understandably live and think from the perspectives of a modern or scientific world-view. Talk about "level" confusion!

Marvin F. Cain, Executive Director at Mid-Columbia Center for Theological Studies, Pasco, Washington writes in his book, *"Jesus the Man"*,

> "In the first centuries of the common era,
> Jesus, as a Jewish teacher/healer/ prophet,
> was intelligible to people who were the heirs
> of the scriptures and traditions of Israel.

However, that Jesus made little sense to Greeks and Romans. As a result, *the early Christians reformulated their message about Jesus into the language of the Greek and Roman gods.* That reformulation reached its climax in the church councils of the fourth and fifth centuries and in the historic creeds of Christianity. *Today, however, many find the Jewish Jesus of the first century more relevant and more intelligible than the Jesus of later Christian dogma* . . . . Antiquated theology, or appeals to creeds or traditions for truth, should be no more acceptable than such appeals would be in the fields of astronomy, physics, or medicine." (Italics mine.)

My point? If Christians could *"reformulate"* the message about Jesus in order to communicate to the people of the fourth and fifth centuries, they can do so today. In fact, that's being done quite effectively outside the "organized church". Movies have succeeded in this extremely well. So have the lyrics and music of popular songwriters and composers. **But better than reformulating beliefs about Jesus, is the current re-discovery of who he truly was and what he actually taught. That's a tremendous story well worth relating!**

When our children graduate from high school they are expected to be proficient in mathematics, the sciences, history, English, and possibly another language. They have been taught many other practical courses including use of a computer. If what they eventually learn about religion is at best on a level of the fifth grade, can you blame many of them for giving up on Sunday School (and the church) upon reaching their teens?

Religion and Spirituality do not rank very high for parents who mainly want material and social success for their children. Why is that so? Obviously since one succeeds economically, without any apparent need for religion. Children are graded only on their understanding *how* the Universe functions but not necessarily *why*. We teach them how to live in this world but not why they live and to what purpose ultimately. **The power of myth and good story telling is absent for the most part in education.**

A long-time personal friend, John C Soller Sr. of Cincinnati, Ohio, in reviewing my first draft of this letter, suggested that I address the angle of "tough love." He wrote:

> "This (tough love) is where I think we, as a generation, have fallen short time and time again. The parents, the courts, the pulpits; all have fallen down tremendously with the advent of the Baby Boomers. Look at us today. Look at the "me generation." Look at how the family has broken down. See the over- populated prisons. See the crap on the movie screens and cable television. Yes, even my media, radio, is reduced to a point that I hardly recognize. And on.

Tough love is where the rubber meets
the road and firm discipline needs to be
enforced."

And I might add, what captivating messages are
currently available to counteract all these social
problems? If the appeal to kids and adults is based
on the lowest common denominator, how do we
present a higher quality of information? Is there not
a more attractive package in the teachings of the
Masters? If what is being taught to our kids has little
practical value in answering their purpose for living
we have only to look to ourselves.

In 1970, together with several clergy, I visited
Israel. We stayed one night at a rural kibutz
bordering on the Sea of Galilee. This farm
community recognized the value of rearing kids,
as well as crops. While the parents worked the
fields, the children were under the tutelage of
professionally trained surrogate caregivers. If,
when Dad and Mom returned from their day's
labors, showing too much stress and strain, then
the surrogate parents had the authority to refuse
them their children until they both, the children,
as well as the parents, could be respected. Quality
bed-time stories seemed to have worked well in
the past.

This is an example of "tough love" which seems
to address one very important ingredient of Love
which is **Self-respect**. A young child's
unconsciousness is as porous as a sponge and soaks
up everything surrounding him. That includes also

the verbal abuse from parents. Small wonder, the gang seems to offer an "acceptable" refuge.

Nevertheless, I am optimistic that many parents, teachers, and grandparents have heard the message and, like John Soller, appreciate that their children are too valuable and vulnerable to be wasted. I believe there are current movies and talk shows which are effectively informing **how** and **why** we can Love one another. Should not the church produce much more relevant educational tools? The time is now for us to be so much more creative as the interpreters and "story tellers" of Holy Words; including the Wisdom of all past Masters! I guarantee that we can choose to engender within our children meaningful Answers about Self-Love; Self-respect, and of equal importance, **why we Live!**

Jesus of Nazareth knew well the writings of *Torah*; the first five books of the Bible. In his teachings, he often referred to the book of *Deuteronomy*, as well as several of the *Prophets*. But the traditions and rituals and purity laws recited there were not as important to him as **Doing and Being what Abba, his Heavenly Father willed; to Do and Be Love with all heart, soul, mind and strength!** The parables and stories Jesus told emphasized this. One of the Old Testament prophets with whom Jesus was familiar, Micah, wrote:

"With what shall I come before the Lord and bow down before the exalted God. Shall I come before him with burnt offerings, with calves a year old? Will the Lord be pleased with thousands of rams, with ten

thousands of rivers of oil? Shall I offer my firstborn for my transgression, the fruit of my body for the sin of my soul? He has showed you, O man, what is good. And what does the Lord require of you? To act justly and to love mercy and to walk humbly with your God."

Just imagine what this world can be when the 25% of its population confessing allegiance to the Christ, takes Jesus seriously and **become the storytellers he invited them to be.** Remember John Lennon? Of course, he was one of the Beatles. His song *Imagine* has had more power on the minds of young people than thousands of Sunday sermons. 'Hear' that music again:

> *Imagine there's no heaven, It's easy if you try,*
> *No hell below us, Above us only sky,*
> *Imagine all the people living for today . . .*
> *Imagine there's no countries, It isn't hard to do,*
> *Nothing to kill or die for, No religion too,*
> *Imagine all the people living life in peace . . .*
> *Imagine no possessions, I wonder if you can,*
> *No need for greed or hunger, A brotherhood of man,*
> *Imagine all the people, sharing all the world . . .*
> *You may say I'm a dreamer, But I'm not the only one,*
> *I hope some day you'll join us, And the world will live as one.*

John Lennon (Bag Productions Inc.)

What a story Lennon sings! It's imaginative is it not?

Think of the **Knowledge, Power, and Presence** world citizens have, as they listen to the Wisdom of the ages propounded by prophets, teachers, poets, artists, celebrities, and musicians. **We live in a time of unlimited potential with each of us capable of telling and singing our amazing stories of Love.**

CHAPTER TEN

"NEW OCCASIONS TEACH NEW DUTIES"

AMONG MY ESTEEMED teachers is John Shelby Spong, the retired Episcopal Bishop of Newark. I have read every one of his books, and received as much inspiration from him as from that other Bishop, John A. T. Robinson. (Robinson wrote *Honest To God* in 1962, the year of my ordination.) Spong, and like minded scholars, credit Robinson' insights for motivating us to rethink our views on Christianity. Spong's *A New Christianity For A New World*, has prompted me to join the growing chorus and numbers of modern protestors wanting to republish what Jesus of Nazareth actually taught.

Spong describes his experience of God in these powerful memorable words:

"I live at this moment inside a powerful experience of the divine, the holy. I call the content of that experience God. I trust its reality. The God that my life has encountered and engaged is most profoundly present for me in the portrait painted by the early church of the man called Jesus of Nazareth. Jesus is thus for me the doorway into this God. His life reflects the life that I call God. His love reflects the love that I call God. His being reveals the Ground of Being that I call God. The God I have met in Jesus calls me to live fully, to love wastefully, and to be all that I can be. When I do all these things, I believe that I make God visible and real for others."

To which I respond, "Wow!" Or, "Amen!" Thank you Bishop Spong!

What the early church taught included more than what 'orthodox' Christianity recognizes today. The creeds of the church, which developed some two to three hundred years after Jesus lived, were adopted after many heated and, yes, even physical skirmishes among bishops and theologians. ("Blood-baths," actually.) Read your history books! The meetings were very unchristian. Politics within church and state were no different then than today! Majority rule settled what would be considered 'orthodox' teaching.

Now hear this please! **'Orthodoxy' and Truth** are not necessarily identical! Any constitutional lawyer can relate how settled holdings of courts are often reversed. What are majority opinions can in time become the minority. What is true for state government is equally true for church government because both are man's interpretations. Neither of those judicatories are Realms of Absolute Truth. What is Truth? "**I AM.**" (**So are We,** *as* **the Image of God!**)

Many people within and without Christianity are saying this! It is time for the institutional church to wake up. The world awaits many more letters of protests from those of us who have been silent much too long! I am proud to be an associate member of the Westar Institute, an advocate for literacy in understanding the Bible & Religion. The Institute says that the separation of church and state is not a license to remain piously ignorant. World renowned scholars have inaugurated a series of *Jesus Seminars on the Road* in order to bridge the gap between the local church parishioner's biblical knowledge and what any high school student is capable of learning. Such was my predicament, referred to earlier when I, fresh out of seminary, failed to challenge the congregation with the Truth I knew. Quite a *mis*-take!

I am reminded of one of my favorite hymns the lyrics of which include these lines by James Russell Lowell, *"New occasions teach new duties; Time makes ancient good uncouth; they must upward still and onward who would keep abreast of truth."* To all my colleagues in ministry, . . . to you I say, "Why should we delay in sharing all this available Knowledge with the millions of our brothers and sisters thirsting for what we have learned? Why our continual hesitancy?" Do we yet lack courage to proclaim boldly the same message as Jesus, our master teacher? How many of us can write this letter? May I suggest hundreds? Thousands? **Will we sit down today with pen in hand, or laptop on knees, and write?**

At the beginning of this letter I wrote that my intentions are personal but not private.

From *A Course in Miracles*, Jesus directs to each of us (should we choose to hear him) a very personal request. He says, *"I am sorry when my brothers do not share my decision to hear only one Voice, because it weakens them as teachers and as learners. Yet I know they cannot really betray themselves or me, and that it is still on them that I must build my church. There is no choice in this, because only you can be the foundation of God's church. A church is where an altar is, and the presence of the altar is what makes the church holy. A church that does not inspire love has a hidden altar that is not serving the purpose for which God intended it. I must found His church on you, because those who accept me as a model are literally my disciples. Disciples are followers, and if the model they follow has chosen to save them pain in all respects, they are unwise not to follow him."* (T.6.I.8 pg 93)

Do me a favor, will you? Read and meditate on those words. I promise that you will hear a Voice personally addressing you. You are the church about which Jesus is speaking. **You are the "altar" of Holiness, Peace, Love, Selfrespect, and Creativity!**

I'm grateful to the people of Community Church of Lauderdale By-The-Sea. In the ten plus years we experienced together, we accepted the premise that Love *is* all there is. We ended our worship services with the Beatles tune, "All You Need is Love." Pastor and people joyously smiling, laughing,—enjoying the conclusion of a celebration of God's Presence, this accompanied by jazz piano, drums, and saxophone/flute!

Community Church's message is simple: *"Teach only Love for that is what you are."* (ACIM) The people are learning how to practice this consciously by avoiding guilt trips for others or themselves. They are not alone.

The ambience of *'Teach only Love'* can be found among scores of like-minded communities arising all over the world. Visit them. You will recognize **IT** immediately upon entering the doors of these guilt free sanctuaries. Their welcome signs are more than a note on the outside signboard. You will be received as one who has more to offer than your money. You will be greeted as one in whom the Christ is seen. Your message will be received as of equal importance, because, what can one choose to share that is of any greater importance than the **Presence of the "I AM" that You Are?**

We are either giving Love or crying out for Love. Since there is no fear in Love we do not hesitate to Do and Be for our neighbor while she is in pain. Whenever I visit someone in the hospital, for example, I do not see him as Being anything but whole; indeed, healthy, holy and perfect. Why would

I want to make real for him his sickness when I do not see him as 'sick'? At the same time, I honor the physician's practice of his art in helping the patient heal. Simultaneously, on the level of Love's Perception, I would mirror back, through Love's Gaze, what each of us sees in the *"I AMNESS"* of our Selves. That is holistic healing!

There is included within Christianity, an 'orthodoxy' of the Eastern Church which I love. Joy defines the liturgy. Services go well beyond just 'an accustomed hour' in order to celebrate joyously the "resurrection" of Jesus. The Western or Roman church, with its emphasis primarily on the crucifixion of Jesus, is obviously of a different character in its liturgical expression. Non-Catholic churches range somewhere between these two. Have you questioned why this might be?

The various churches are separated on the basis of doctrinal differences in the same way as nations establish artificial boundaries. Do you suppose that Jesus of Nazareth ever intended that his followers would emulate nation-states? Matthew's Gospel has Jesus calling his disciples together telling them not to *"Lord it over others like the rulers and high officials."* He advises them to become as servants in the same manner as he is a servant. That was the true greatness of Mother Teresa. The master teacher,Jesus, even went so far as to correct anyone for calling him great. *"Only God is Great,"* said he. Furthermore, he promised his followers that they, themselves, would be capable of *"Doing greater deeds"* than he. Such is the "Church" he intended!

Jesus said if we want peace on Earth then we have to teach Peace to learn it. Think about that for a moment. Do the leaders of the world want peace if they teach war? For them, the name of the game is power. In fact, war colleges are where we learn the 'art' of war. Yet, our most famous generals remind us that war is hell. How insane we are.

But, goes the argument, were it not for strong armies and superior weapons we would not be free. History records that empires come and go. None last forever. The human race has for several thousands of years gradually evolved to the present world crises where humanity itself survives only if its leaders choose Peace instead of war. Were it not for wiser and cooler heads, we probably would not be alive today to even discuss the options. (The Cuban Crisis, for example; or possibly, Iraq, and North Korea?)

As I drive on the crowded super highways at speeds exceeding posted limits, I think of all the possible accidents that are avoided because of the sanity of most of the drivers. There are, of course, the tragic losses of life due to the occasional reckless, or suicidal, driver. For nearly 99.99% of the time that we are at risk, we arrive home safely. There is also deeply embedded within our unconscious the will to survive in spite of occasional lapses into insanity. I sincerely believe that Mankind has arrived at a point where we **are awaking** into a Conscious awareness that the only Road worth traveling today is the Road marked **Love and Peace.**

The true story of a remarkable woman named

Peace Pilgrim best summarizes the practicality of what we are urging. I have the permission of her friends to quote the following:

"Between 1953 and 1981, Peace Pilgrim walked more than 25,000 miles across the United States spreading her simple peace message. Carrying in her tunic pockets her only possessions, she vowed, 'I shall remain a wanderer until mankind has learned the way of peace, walking until given shelter and fasting until given food.' She talked with people on dusty roads and city streets, to church, college, civic groups, on TV and radio, discussing peace within and peace in the world.

"Her pilgrimage covered the entire peace picture: peace among nations, groups, individuals, and the very important inner peace — because that is where peace really begins.

"She believed world peace would come *when enough people attain* **inner peace**. Her life and work show that **one person with inner peace** can make a significant contribution to world peace." (Italics and darkening mine.)

She and Jesus of Nazareth truly walked the talk. Will the followers of Jesus hit the road today and sway the leaders of nations to know war no more? (i.e. all 1,500,000,000 followers of the Prince of Peace?) Peace Pilgrim purposely changed her given and surnames in order to manifest clearly her intentions. She was killed in an automobile accident. Ironically, throughout her previous 25,000 mile walk, she had never before accepted a ride.

Do we not hear 25% of the common people of the world crying out for the "Love of Christ?" . . . i.e. Christians who sing "Onward Christian Soldiers marching as to war . . ." (*correction*-**Love and Peace**). Are they not persuasive enough to declare that the message of Jesus, the Galilean Peasant, is solely about a Love and Peace reaching beyond the 'ego' level? Equally of importance, let's also hear the other 75% of the common people since each **of us is called to the same understanding!** Some are asserting today "Now is the Hour of Power." The world awaits this Knowledge, Power, Peace and Love among all nations.

Back at Community Church, I hear the voices of people singing with millions of others those familiar words: *"**Let there be Peace on Earth, and let it begin with me.**"*

BIBLIOGRAPHY

The Holy Bible—New International Version, International Bible Society, 1984

A Course In Miracles—Foundation for A Course in Miracles 2nd Ed. 1992

Borg, Marcus—*God at 2000*, Epilogue: Reflections by Marcus Borg, Morehouse, 2000

Cain, Marvin F—*Jesus The Man*, An Introduction for People at Home in the Modern World; Polebridge Press, Santa Rosa, Cal., 1999

Cohen, Alan—*The Dragon Doesn't Live Here Anymore*, Alan Cohen Programs and Publications, Haiku, Hi.

Douglas-Klotz, Neil—*The Hidden Gospel,* Decoding the Spiritual Message of the The Aramaic Jesus; The Theosophical Society of America, 1999

Lennon, John—*Imagine*, Bag Productions, Inc.

Mundy, Jon—*The Missouri Mystic*, and publisher of *Miracles* magazine, Campbell Hall, N.Y. 10916 (39 Hickory Dr.)

Nasr, Seyyed Hossein, *God at 2000*, God: The Reality to Serve, Love and Know; Morehouse, 2000

Pilgrim, Peace—*Her Life and Work In Her Own Words*, Ocean Tree Books, 1991

Scott, Bernard Brandon—*Re-Imagine The World*, Polebridge Press, Santa Rosa, 2001

Spong, John Shelby—*A New Christianity For A New World*, How A New Faith Is Being Born; HarperSan Francisco, 2001

Spong, John Shelby—*The War With Iraq: Can we find unity in our Humanity*, an Essay published by Agora Media, Inc. 2002

Tolle, Eckhart—*The Power of Now*, A Guide to Spiritual Enlightenment; New World Library, 1999

Yonan Codex Foundation, Inc.—*Enlightenment . . . From the Aramaic*, Atlanta, Ga. 1974